Dress-up Dolls

Perfect Princesses

igloobooks

It was a very special day at Cupcake Castle. It was Princess Holly's birthday and everybody had got up early to start preparing a birthday party for Holly, her sister Poppy and all of Holly's friends.

Princess Holly was so excited about her birthday. She burst into her sister, Poppy's bedroom, as she was brushing her hair.

"It's my birthday today and I'm going have a party!" said Princess Holly.

"I know! Happy birthday, Holly!" laughed Princess Poppy, as she gave Holly a birthday card. "We are going to have such a fantastic day. Are we still going to have a secret sleepover party later, too?"

"Of course!" said Princess Holly, "I can't wait!"

Press out the clothes and help the girls get dressed. Don't forget Princess Holly's birthday card!

After a special birthday breakfast, Princess Holly and Princess Poppy decided to go for a walk in the royal grounds.

"We'd better put our shawls on," said Princess Poppy. "We don't want to catch colds on your birthday."

The princesses ran in and out of the trees, playing hide and seek.

"Look at these butterflies, Poppy. They're so pretty," said Princess Holly.

Find the princesses' shawls.
Look carefully for their
shoes and crowns, too.

They chased the butterflies as they flitted and fluttered on the breeze.
Before they realised it, they'd chased them all the way back to the
castle gardens. The butterflies flew away as the princesses stopped
for a rest.

"Let's go and see how our seeds are growing," suggested Princess Holly.
"We haven't looked at them for a while."

The princesses popped into the summer house and got changed into their gardening clothes.

"It's very muddy, isn't it? I'm so glad we're wearing our wellies," laughed Princess Poppy.

They walked across the gardens to their own special flower beds.

"Oh look, Poppy! Our little seedlings have grown into beautiful flowers," said Princess Holly. She sniffed the biggest flower she could see. "Mmm, and they smell gorgeous, too."

The girls stood back and admired the blooms for a few moments.
Then they heard a familiar noise. Plip! Plop! Plip! Plop!

Look for the princesses'
gardening clothes
and pretty wellies.
Princess Poppy needs
her watering can, too!

"Oh no! It's started to rain," shrieked Princess Holly. "Quick, let's run back to the castle."

Back at the castle, the chef was preparing the food for Princess Holly's birthday party.

"Can we help, please?" asked Princess Poppy. "We'll try not to make a mess."

The princesses put their aprons on and Chef showed them how to decorate some cupcakes with icing and sugar stars.

Dress Princess Holly and Princess Poppy in their aprons and hats so they can decorate the cupcakes.

Splat!

"Whoops! I'm so sorry!" said Princess Poppy, as she squeezed lots of pink icing all over the cupcakes.

"Oh no, Poppy! Maybe we should leave the chef to ice the cupcakes on his own," laughed Princess Holly.

The girls ran out of the kitchens and up the sweeping staircase to Princess Holly's dressing room.

"It's nearly time for your party, Holly. Let's try some dresses on," said Princess Poppy.

The princesses tried on lots of different party dresses, crowns and shoes.

"I can't decide which to wear," said Princess Poppy. "They're all lovely."

Princesses Holly and Poppy love trying on pretty dresses. Find their gowns, shoes, crowns and bags and create your favourite combination!

Soon, it was time for Princess Holly's party. One by one, her friends arrived, carrying lots of presents and cards.

Princess Holly was wearing her best pink dress, decorated with layers of lace and on her head she wore a jewelled crown. Princess Poppy's dress was sparkling purple, with bows around the hem.

"Here come the cakes, said Princess Poppy. Don't they look wonderful?"

"Mine's not very pretty. I think I must have one that you decorated!" laughed Princess Holly.

Happy Birthday, Holly!

Look for the princesses' dresses. Don't forget Princess Holly's presents and cards!

Holly

Soon the party was over and it was time for Princess Holly's friends to go home. Princess Holly and Princess Poppy went up to Poppy's bedroom while the maids cleared up downstairs.

The princesses brushed their hair, cleaned their teeth and put on their royal nighties.

"I'm so very tired," said Princess Poppy, "but we've had such a wonderful time celebrating your birthday. Now, shall I go and see if there are any cakes left over for our secret sleepover party?"

But Princess Holly didn't reply. She was already fast asleep!

Help get the princesses ready for bed. Can you find their pretty nighties and slippers?

Design your own princess outfits!

Why not create your own special outfits for Princess Holly and Princess Poppy? Use these templates to help you design some pretty dresses, shoes and accessories for them to wear. Try to be as creative and imaginative as you can!

Trace the shape of the clothes onto some card, then design a pattern and draw it onto your outfit.

Use pens, pencils and glitter to decorate the clothes and accessories.

Ask an adult to help you cut out the shapes. You're now ready to dress the princesses in your own designs.

Holly

Dress-up Dolls

Fluttering Fairies

Best friends, Milly and Daisy, lived in Fairyland, in a toadstool house on the edge of a magical forest.

They both loved baking and had got up early to make special treats – fairy cakes!

"Mmm, these smell delicious!" said Milly, as she took the cakes out of the oven. "But they're too hot to eat at the moment. Let's go and fly around the forest while we wait for the cakes to cool."

Press out Milly and Daisy's clothes. Can you find their pretty aprons, matching hats and wooden spoons?

Milly and Daisy took off their aprons and flew out of the toadstool and into the forest.

"Look, Milly," said Daisy excitedly, as she pointed to a poster pinned to a tree trunk. "There's going to be a Fairy Woodland Ball tonight, right here in the forest."

Find the princesses' dresses. Look carefully for their pretty wands and shoes, too.

"That sounds magical," replied Milly. "Let's go and ask all our fairy friends if they want to come too."

Fairy Woodland Ball
Here tonight!

Milly and Daisy put on their warm, fluffy coats and hats and flew above the treetops to Fairy Winterland, to visit their friends, the snow fairies.

Some of the snow fairies were filling acorn shells with a mixture of snow and juice and one snow fairy was carving blocks of ice with her wand.

Milly and Daisy are lovely and warm.
Press out their fluffy coats and matching hats.
Can you find their cosy boots, too?

Milly and Daisy told the snow fairies about the ball and asked them if they wanted to go.

"We heard about it earlier today," said one of the snow fairies. "We're all going and we're making magical slush drinks for the party and some pretty ice sculptures for decoration."

"Brilliant!" said Milly. "We'll see you there."

Next, Milly and Daisy fluttered on the breeze to see the rainbow fairies, who were busy painting pieces of card in wonderful, bright, rainbow colours.

"Quick, put these painting overalls on," one of the rainbow fairies said to Milly and Daisy. "We don't want your pretty dresses to get messy."

"What are you doing?" asked Daisy.

"We're making decorations for tonight's ball," said the fairy.
"I hope you and Milly will be going."

Milly and Daisy picked up a brush each and helped the rainbow fairies with their painting.

"The forest will look so pretty tonight with the decorations in the trees," said Milly.

Find Milly and Daisy's painting clothes, so that they can help make decorations. Don't forget their paint pots and brushes.

On their way back to the forest, Milly and Daisy visited the flower fairies.

"Are you going to the Fairy Woodland Ball tonight?" asked Milly.

"Oh, yes, we can't wait," replied one of the flower fairies. "We've been making dresses all morning. Here, try these on."

Milly and Daisy tried on lots of pretty dresses and dainty headbands decorated with tiny delicate flowers.

"These are all so beautiful, I feel like a fairy princess," said Daisy.

Milly and Daisy loved trying on the pretty dresses that the flower fairies have made. Look carefully for their shoes and headbands, too.

Evening soon arrived and it was time for the ball.

Milly had chosen to wear a wonderful dress layered with pink, scented rose petals and matching shoes. Daisy's dress was, of course, covered in lots of little daisies and her wand had a dainty daisy chain wrapped around it.

They also took with them the fairy cakes they'd baked that morning to share with everyone.

"Oh, this place looks so magical!" Milly gasped, as she and Daisy fluttered down to join the party.

All the girls' fairy friends were there and together they all spent a wonderful evening dancing and giggling.

Find the fairies' party dresses. Can you pick out their matching wands and shoes, too?

Before they knew it, the ball was over. Milly and Daisy helped tidy up and it was soon time to go home to bed.

The girls took off their wonderful dresses and put on their fairy nighties. In the distance, an owl hooted as the girls got into bed.

Find Milly and Daisy's nighties and slippers and dress the fairies ready for bed. Don't forget their teddies!

"What a wonderful evening," said Milly. "But now we should go to sleep. It's well past our bedtime."

"Goodnight, Milly," said Daisy.

"Sleep tight, Daisy," replied Milly.

Design your own fairy outfits!

Why not create some of your own special outfits for Daisy and Milly? Use the templates below to help you design some pretty dresses and shoes for the fairies to wear. Try to be as creative and imaginative as you can.

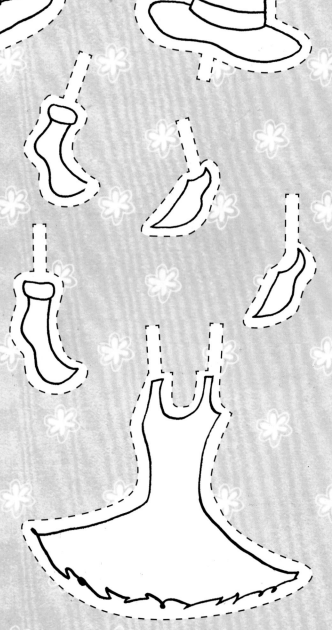

Trace the shape of the clothes onto some card, then design a pattern and draw it onto your outfit.

Use pens, pencils and glitter to decorate the clothes and shoes.

Ask an adult to help you cut out the shapes. You're now ready to dress the fairies in your own designs.

Dress-up Dolls
Brilliant Ballerinas

Lauren and Olivia loved ballet. They went to lessons whenever they could and hoped that one day they would become famous ballerinas.

The girls were never late for a lesson and today was no exception. As they arrived, the teacher gathered all the ballerinas together and said she had an important announcement to make.

Press out the clothes and help Lauren and Olivia get dressed. Don't forget their kit bags!

"We are going to put on a performance. I'll teach you some routines and you'll need to wear special costumes."

"How exciting!" said Lauren. "We've never been in a proper show before."

Lauren and Olivia changed out of their clothes. They put on their leotards, leg warmers and practice skirts and skipped into the ballet studio to join the other ballerinas.

As the girls did their warm-up stretches the teacher asked them to think about which show they'd like to perform.

Dress Lauren and Olivia in their pretty leotards and practice skirts. Remember to give them their water!

Lauren and Olivia moved their feet and arms into the different ballet positions and pirouetted and leapt until they were worn out.

"I wonder what performance we should do," said Olivia as they stopped to have a drink. "Maybe we should look at some costumes for ideas."

As soon as they had finished their lesson, Lauren and Olivia went into one of the costume rooms. They admired the beautiful tutus hanging in a row and found a big box full of props and headdresses covered in jewels.

"Wow!" gasped Lauren. "There are some wonderful outfits here. Let's try some on."

Lauren tried on a lilac tutu which sparkled with sequins and beads and Olivia found a tutu with layers of netting and flowers sewn in to it.

They tried on headdresses to match and satin shoes with long, silky ribbons.

Lauren and Olivia loved trying on the beautiful costumes. Find their pretty tutus, tiaras and satin shoes.

Lauren and Olivia went to look for their friends. The other ballerinas had found more dresses in another room.

"Look! Here are the costumes from Sleeping Beauty," one of the other ballerinas said. "Why don't you try them on?"

Look for the ballerinas' pretty Sleeping Beauty costumes. Don't forget Olivia's magic wand!

Lauren tried on a pink dress decorated with crystals and feathers and Olivia tried on a blue one.

"These are very pretty, but the feathers keep tickling me!" laughed Lauren.

"Me too," giggled Olivia. "Maybe we should go and look for more costumes to try on."

Lauren and Olivia found a room that they had never been inside before. Olivia peered around the door and squealed with excitement at the rows of costumes hanging up. They tried on new outfits and took a magic wand each from the props box.

"Look, Olivia! I'm the Sugar Plum Fairy from The Nutcracker." Lauren said, as she twirled around the room.

"And I'm Tinkerbell from Peter Pan," replied Olivia.

Can you find the Sugar Plum Fairy outfit and the Tinkerbell costume? Don't forget the headdresses!

PROPS

The girls continued to look through the rails of outfits. They tried on many dresses before finally telling the ballet teacher which show they had chosen to perform.

"What a great choice," said their teacher. "We'd better start rehearsing right away."

Over the next few weeks, the ballerinas rehearsed as often as they could and it was soon the day of the performance.

"We just need to have one final rehearsal before changing into our costumes," Lauren said to the other ballerinas.

They all put on their practice tutus and crossover cardigans and danced the routine one last time.

"I think we're ready now," said Olivia. "Let's do our make up and put our costumes on."

Ballet positions
1st
2nd
3rd
4th
5th

Look carefully for the ballerinas' practice tutus and cardigans, so that they can rehearse their performance one last time.

In the theatre the audience sat down and the lights were dimmed.

The ballerinas had chosen to perform Cinderella. Lauren was playing the lead and Olivia was the Fairy Godmother.

Help the ballerinas get dressed for the show! They'll need their costumes, shoes and headdresses. Don't forget Olivia's wand!

The audience cheered and clapped as the ballerinas started their routines. Lauren and Olivia moved their arms gracefully as they skipped and leapt across the stage in their wonderful costumes.

"This is fantastic!" Lauren whispered to Olivia, as they danced together. "Don't you just love being a ballerina?"

Design your own ballerina costumes!

Why not create some of your own special outfits for Lauren and Olivia? Use these templates to help you design some pretty costumes for the ballerinas to wear. Try to be as creative and imaginative as you can!

Trace the shape of the clothes onto some card, then design a pattern and draw it onto your outfit.

Use pens, pencils and glitter to decorate the skirts and tops.

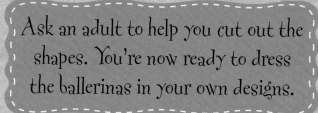

Ask an adult to help you cut out the shapes. You're now ready to dress the ballerinas in your own designs.

"Hello! My name is Milly. Press out this picture of me, choose some pretty outfits and dress me up!" Milly x

"Hello! I'm Daisy. Press out this picture of me and dress me up in my beautiful fairy outfits!" Daisy x